KITCHEN WIZARD COOKBOOK

by DEBORAH JARVIS

illustrated by Arthur Robins

SCHOLASTIC BOOK SERVICES

NEW YORK • TORONTO • LONDON • AUCKLAND • SYDNEY • TOKYO

To Wizard's editor—
who never once complained of indigestion

ISBN 0-590-31302-9

Copyright © Deborah Jarvis 1977. Copyright © Illustrations Arthur Robins, 1977. This edition is published in the United States by Scholastic Books Services, a Division of Scholastic Magazines, Inc., 50 West 44 Street, New York, N.Y. 10036, by arrangement with William Collins Sons & Company Ltd.

12 11 10 9 8 7 6 5 4 3 2 1   9   0 1 2 3 4 5/8

Contents

A Message
from the Kitchen Wizard

There are recipes for mixtures and potions in this
book to suit your every mood. You can join Huck Finn
for a picnic on the Mississippi. Or munch a brunch
with the Munchkins in the marvelous Land of Oz. Or
make weird Blackberry Witches or creamy delicious
Polar Bear Sandwiches.

But before you dabble in the delights of kitchen wizardry, have a look at the words of wiz-dom in the next few pages. The High Council of Kitchen Wizards warns against stirring up magical mixtures before first reading instructions and recipes all the way through.

So put on your wizard cap and start your kitchen wizardry by brushing up on Basic Abracadabra (see pages 6 to 13). Remember: magic works both ways!

Basic Abracadabra

ALWAYS get permission from the senior chef in your house to use the kitchen — and ask him or her to stand by while you cook — just in case you need an extra hand or help with testing and tasting.

BAKE: cooking in the oven.

BEAT: mixing vigorously with a circular motion to make a mixture smooth. You can use a hand beater or a spoon.

BLEND: mixing two or more ingredients together until you can't tell one from the other.

BOIL: heating a liquid until it bubbles furiously.

COLLECT all the ingredients and equipment you need for a recipe before you start to cook.

CREAM: Beating sugar and soft butter with a spoon until light and fluffy. Sit down to do this and hold the bowl in your lap. 7

DICE: cutting into small squares. Use cutting board and always cut down, away from your fingers.

EVEN super chefs try to cover up, so wear an apron when you cook.

FOLD: mixing a light ingredient into a heavier one. Use a metal spoon and gently cut into mixture with edge of spoon, moving down across bottom of bowl, and up over the surface.

FRY: cooking in hot fat in a frying pan on top of the stove.

GRATE: cutting into tiny pieces by rubbing against holes in grater.

GREASE: rubbing oil or butter on cooking pans to prevent sticking. Use a piece of wax paper.

HOLDING a measuring cup in the air won't give an accurate reading. Always put cup down on a flat surface and read at eye level.

IF you keep the sink full of hot soapy water while you're cooking, you can put dirty spoons and bowls right in. Saves space and cuts washing-up time.

JUST before you finish mixing, quickly read through the recipe to make sure you haven't left anything out.

KEEP the handles of pots turned in — not sticking out over the edge of the stove, where they can be bumped and tip over.

LEVEL off ingredients in cups, tablespoons, and teaspoons with the back of a knife or a spatula.

MELT: turning a solid ingredient into a liquid by heating in a saucepan on top of the stove.

NUTS can be chopped without a knife. Crush them in their bag or in a cloth with a rolling pin or small hammer.

ONLY a few inches can make a big difference in your baking. Always try to use the size baking pan suggested in the recipe.

PUT on oven mitts every time you take a hot pot off the stove or out of the oven.

QUICK way to stir a liquid into a dry mixture: Make a well, or hole, in the center of the dry ingredients. Pour liquid in and then carefully stir around and around from the center until it is all mixed in.

REMEMBER to cool cakes, breads, and cookies on a wire rack. They will get soggy if you cool them in the pan.

SIFT: put flour or other dry ingredients through a sieve to get rid of lumps.

SIMMER: cooking liquid in a saucepan over low heat so that it bubbles very slowly.

TBSP = tablespoon

TSP = teaspoon

TIE back long hair.

TOOTHPICK TEST: If a toothpick stuck into a cake comes out dry, then the cake is ready to take out of the oven.

UNWATCHED pots can burn or boil over, so never leave anything cooking on the stove unless you are in the kitchen to watch it.

VERY cool bowls and beaters will make it easier to whip cream. Before starting a recipe with whipped cream, put the bowl and the beater in the refrigerator to chill.

WOODEN spoons are whizz-sticks when it comes to stirring hot things. They will never burn your fingers the way a metal spoon can.

X-TRA points to kitchen wizards who know that 3 teaspoons = 1 tablespoon; 8 ounces = 1 cup; 2 cups = 1 pint.

YOLKS and whites of eggs are easily separated this way.

ZIP through the washing up, whistle around the counter tops with a damp cloth, and you'll be the most popular kitchen wizard ever.

13

A Munchkin Brunch

Even though brunch is part breakfast and part lunch, the Munchkins like eating it any time of day. And if you go to the Land of Oz, they won't mind sharing it with you either. In an instant, you will have a glass of milk in one hand and a double helping of Crunchy-Brunchy in the other.

Thanks to Dorothy, it is no longer necessary to kill a witch or arrive by cyclone to enjoy a Munchkin brunch. It just takes a few lessons from the Wizard himself...

Crunchy-Brunchy

It is impossible to eat Crunchy-Brunchy quietly, and that is why the Munchkins like it so much. With a supply of raisins, nuts, and oatmeal, you can sample it yourself and find out what all the noise is about.

SECRET INGREDIENTS

MAGIC FORMULA

1. Preheat oven to 450°.

2. Grease a small cookie sheet.

3. Melt together in a large saucepan over low heat and stir until sugar is dissolved. ——— 3 tbsp butter
5 tbsp brown sugar
2½ tbsp honey

4. Remove pan from heat and mix in thoroughly ——— 2 cups uncooked oatmeal
½ cup raisins
¼ cup chopped nuts

5. Spread mixture on greased cookie sheet and bake until well-browned. Take pan out and set it aside to cool.

6. Crumble Crunchy-Brunchy into small pieces with your hands. Store in a tightly closed can or plastic bag.

7. Serve in a bowl with lots of cold milk or eat as a snack.

Flying Monkey Muffins

Long ago in the Land of Oz, there was a magic golden cap which granted three wishes to the wearer. These wishes were carried out by a strange band of flying monkeys. Though the cap has been lost, and the monkeys have not been seen for years, the Munchkins keep dreaming up ways of enticing them back.

These muffins, dressed up to look like flying monkeys, are a Munchkin favorite.

SECRET INGREDIENTS

MAGIC FORMULA

1. Fry until crispy_____ 8 strips of bacon
   then drain on a paper towel.

2. Cut in half_____ 2 English muffins
   and toast well.

3. Butter each half,
   then spread with _____ peanut butter

4. Crumble 1 strip of bacon on top of each muffin. Cut remaining strips in half and put 2 halves for wings on each muffin. Use peanuts for eyes and tail.

5. Put Flying Monkeys on a cookie sheet and toast under the broiler until peanut butter is bubbling. Serve at once.

Blackberry Witches

The only thing that could spoil a Munchkin brunch was the arrival of the Wicked Witch of the East. With one swoop of her broom, she would upset the milk and then drop spiders in the peanut butter. You can imagine the cheers when Dorothy's house landed on her, leaving nothing but a pair of silver shoes!

Just to remind themselves how lucky they are to be rid of this wicked woman, the Munchkins eat Blackberry Witch pancakes every other Friday.

SECRET INGREDIENTS

BLACKBERRIES
OR BLUEBERRIES

COOKING OIL

PAN CAKE MIX

LARGE

MAGIC FORMULA

1. Drain berries (save the juice).

2. Pour into mixing bowl _____ ⅔ cup pancake mix

3. Gradually stir in _____ ½ cup berry juice
   1 beaten egg
   1 tbsp oil

4. Blend into batter _____ ⅔ cup blackberries
   or blueberries

5. Pour batter into a pitcher.

6. Wipe the inside of a frying pan with cooking oil and put on medium heat.

7. Pan is hot enough for cooking if drops of water sizzle and bounce, but don't disappear in steam. Then pour small amounts of batter into the frying pan.

8. Turn once, and when golden brown on both sides, lift witches out with a pancake turner. Put them on a plate in the oven (170°) to keep warm until serving. Grease pan again if necessary.

9. Sprinkle with sugar or spread with Honey Butter (see page 23).

Honey Butter

Munchkins are fond of eating Blackberry Witches with Honey Butter. When they fancy a Witch with a bit more spice to it, they whip up a bowl or two of Cinnamon Honey Butter. If it is an extra special occasion, they will make a little Maple Honey Butter.

SECRET INGREDIENTS

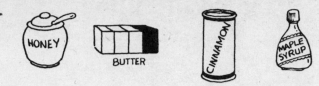

MAGIC FORMULA

1. In a small bowl, use a
   fork to whip _____ 3 tbsp soft butter
   until light and fluffy.

2. Blend in gradually about _____ 5 tbsp honey
   (1 tbsp at a time) and whip
   until smooth and shiny.

CINNAMON HONEY BUTTER
3. Blend in _____ 1¼ heaping tsp
                                               cinnamon

MAPLE HONEY BUTTER
3. Blend in ½ tsp at a time _____ 2½ tsp maple syrup
   until well blended.

4. Use at once or put into a tightly covered jar and
   keep in the refrigerator. (Leave at room temperature
   for 15 minutes before using.) Delicious on toast and
   Witches.

Lunch in Lilliput

When Gulliver was washed up on the beach of Lilliput he terrified the inhabitants. No wonder. He was twelve times their size! Their first reaction was to fasten this giant to the ground before he could do any damage.

With ladders and truckloads of rope, they tied him down. Then just for good measure they bombarded him with arrows. It took some time for Gulliver to convince the Lilliputians that he had no intention of waging war against them. Then they did their best to make Gulliver feel at home.

An imperial commission was set up by the Emperor of Lilliput to see that the man-mountain was well looked after. By order of His Majesty, every village within 900 yards was obliged to deliver meat, fruit, and wine to Gulliver's doorstep every morning. Three hundred cooks prepared his food; 600 Lilliputians were kept busy at his domestic chores; and over 300 tailors set to work to make him a suit of clothes.

If you were suddenly to shrink to a size of barely six inches, it might be helpful to know what a Lilliputian lunch tastes like....

Food Arrows

It wasn't long before the Lilliputians found that the arrows they were shooting at Gulliver were an excellent way of transporting food to the friendly giant's mouth.

SECRET INGREDIENTS

MAGIC FORMULA

1. Drain the pineapple chunks (save the juice). Dice the cheese into 1-inch squares. Cut each piece of ham into four strips.

2. Put a square of cheese at one end of each ham strip and roll up tightly.

3. On each toothpick, thread a pineapple chunk, a piece of rolled-up ham and cheese, and then another pineapple chunk.

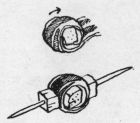

ARROW GLAZE

4. Mix together in small saucepan _____ and stir over low heat until sugar is dissolved. Let mixture boil gently, stirring occasionally, until syrupy.

   2½ tbsp pineapple juice
   2½ tbsp water
   2½ tbsp brown sugar
   1½ tbsp honey

5. Place arrows close together in a baking pan. Spoon arrow glaze over each one.

6. Put the pan under the broiler for about 5 minutes, until ham is slightly browned. Serve at once.

WHIZZ TRICK

To make the arrows look really authentic, serve them from a red apple target. Wash and polish a large red apple, stand it on a plate, and stick the arrows into it.

Triple Glumgluffs

The Lilliputians measured things in glumgluffs, which is about an inch. Gulliver noticed that each meat loaf the cooks brought him for lunch was exactly the size of three glumgluffs. So he named these tempting loaves Triple Glumgluffs.

SECRET INGREDIENTS

MAGIC FORMULA

1. Preheat oven to 425°.

2. Mix together _____ with a fork in a large bowl.

- 1 pound ground beef
- 1 egg
- 1 slice bread, torn into pieces
- 1¼ tbsp dried onion flakes
- 1¼ tsp salt
- ½ tsp pepper

3. With your hands (wash first), shape mixture into small loaves and place on a rack in a roasting pan.

4. In a small bowl, mix _____ together.

- 3½ tbsp ketchup
- 1¼ heaping tbsp brown sugar
- 1¼ tbsp water
- 1¼ tbsp honey
- 1¼ tbsp vinegar
- ½ tbsp mild mustard
- 1¼ tsp Worcestershire sauce

5. Spread sauce over top and sides of each loaf.

6. Bake for 15–20 minutes (or until cooked through). Serve hot or cold.

Empress Tarts

The Empress of Lilliput frequently paid Gulliver social calls, accompanied by her ladies-in-waiting. On these occasions she used to bring delicious lemon, chocolate, and butterscotch tarts from the palace kitchens. She would have a small corner of one with her tea, while Gulliver polished off all the rest in one mouthful.

SECRET INGREDIENTS

MAGIC FORMULA

1. Preheat oven to 350°, and line a muffin pan with cupcake liners. Recipe makes 12 tarts.

2. Put into a plastic bag _____ 22 Graham crackers tie tightly, and crush to fine crumbs with rolling pin.

3. Shake crumbs into a small bowl and blend in _____ ¼ cup butter

4. Coat each cupcake liner with crumbs by pressing firmly into the bottom and sides with the back of a teaspoon.

5. Put the cupcake pan into the refrigerator and chill for at least 15 minutes.

FILLING (Lemon, Chocolate or Butterscotch)

6. Follow directions on _____ 1 small package instant pudding

MERINGUE

7. Beat until standing in soft peaks — 3 egg whites
Beat in (1 tbsp at a time) _____ 8 tbsp sugar
Continue beating until stiff and glossy.

8. Take cupcake pan out of refrigerator and fill each cup ⅔ full with pudding mixture.

9. Then heap meringue on top, making sure it seals in the filling by covering all the edges.

10. Bake 15 to 18 minutes or until meringue is lightly browned.

11. Take out of oven and, when pan is cool, put into refrigerator. Let tarts set for an hour before removing.

A Huckleberry Finn Raft Picnic

As far as Huckleberry Finn was concerned, there wasn't anything nicer than a raft picnic. Tom Sawyer agreed, especially when he managed to slip out of school without being seen and raided Aunt Polly's larder without being caught.

No one knows exactly what a raft picnic is because it has always been a top Finn-Sawyer secret. But it doesn't necessarily have to take place on a raft — or on a boat at all. All you need are one or two rather special ingredients...

Hobo Roll-Ups

Huck was the envy of all the other boys. He swam when it suited him and he didn't care a hoot about school. His trousers, always rolled up to the knees, were the perfect length for fishing and fence climbing.

These sandwiches, which seemed to turn up on every raft picnic, looked so much like Huck's trousers that they were always called Hobo Roll-Ups.

SECRET INGREDIENTS

MAGIC FORMULA

1. Line broiler tray with aluminum foil.

2. Cut crusts off
   and toast _____ 4 slices of bread

3. Butter one side of toast
   and cover with _____ 1 slice cheese
   1 slice ham (on top)

4. Cook in broiler (about 350°) until ham is slightly browned and cheese is bubbling underneath.

5. Let cool for a few minutes, then roll each one up like a jelly roll. Stick a toothpick through the center to hold it together.

6. Put on a plate and serve at once. Remind everyone eating Roll-Ups to remove the toothpicks first, of course.

WHIZZ TRICK

Huck and Tom used the crusts as bait for fishing. You might prefer to put them in a jar and use them to make breadcrumbs (delicious on top of Mountain Soup, p. 47).

Barefoot Bread

Tom and Huck didn't care much for "fancy fixin's," so packing up for a picnic meant taking the easiest things possible. Cornmeal, which they used for making this bread, was the best to carry because it could be stuffed into their pockets.

You can make Barefoot Bread in a frying pan over an open fire or in a baking pan in the oven, depending on your picnic site.

SECRET INGREDIENTS

MAGIC FORMULA

1. Preheat oven to 425°.

2. Grease an 8-inch square baking pan with high sides.

3. Sift together _____ into large bowl
   - ⅔ cup flour
   - ⅔ cup cornmeal
   - 5 tbsp sugar
   - 3 tsp baking powder
   - 1¼ tsp salt

4. Melt in small saucepan over low heat _____ 3 tbsp butter

5. In a small bowl, beat lightly _____ 1 egg

6. Pour melted butter and beaten egg into flour mixture with _____ ¾ cup milk Mix only until flour is blended in. Don't beat.

7. Pour batter into greased pan and bake for 20–25 minutes or until done (use toothpick test).

8. Serve piping hot, sliced, and spread with butter.

WHIZZ TRICK

To make Skillet Bread, grease a large, covered frying pan, and put over low heat to warm until you are ready to use it. Then pour in batter and cook over low heat for about 30 minutes.

Hickory Chicken

Raft picnics tended to be spur of the moment things, so planning for them was practically impossible. Tom had to make last-minute raids on Aunt Polly's larder. On one memorable occasion, he squeezed four pieces of chicken into his back pocket. These were received with great relish by Huck, who rolled them in melted butter and cooked them instantly over the fire.

SECRET INGREDIENTS

4 CHICKEN PIECES   BUTTER

MAGIC FORMULA

1. Preheat oven to 400°.

2. Put into a plastic bag about _____ 2 oz. potato
   tie tightly, and crush with   chips
   rolling pin.

3. Melt in small frying pan _____ 4½ tbsp butter
   Remove pan from heat.

4. Roll chicken pieces in melted
   butter, then drop one at a time
   into bag with potato chip crumbs.
   Hold bag tightly with one hand.
   Shake well until chicken is
   covered in crumbs.

5. Place chicken in a baking pan, skin side up. Pour
   what's left of the melted butter and crumbs over
   the chicken pieces in the pan. Shake a little salt,
   pepper, and paprika over each piece.

6. Bake for 1 hour.

WHIZZ TRICK

    Vary the kind of potato chip you use: Try bacon,
onion, or cheese.

Playin' Hookey Cookies

One whiff of these cookies baking in the oven and Tom knew it was time for a picnic. There was nothing he could do to stop his feet from going straight to the kitchen, and before you could say Jack Robinson, he had hooked half a dozen (the recipe makes about 30) from right under Aunt Polly's nose.

SECRET INGREDIENTS

MAGIC FORMULA

1. Preheat oven to 350°.

2. Lightly grease a large cookie sheet.

3. Cream together _____ in large mixing bowl until light and fluffy.
   - ½ cup soft butter
   - ½ cup crunchy peanut butter

4. Add gradually _____ to butter mixture.
   - ½ cup granulated sugar
   - ½ cup brown sugar

5. Beat in _____
   - 1 egg
   - ½ tsp vanilla

6. Sift in, mixing well _____
   - 1 cup flour
   - 1 tsp baking powder
   - pinch of salt

7. Flour hands lightly and roll dough into small balls (about the size of walnuts). Place on cookie sheet about 2 inches apart. Flatten dough with a floured fork.

8. Bake 12 – 15 minutes. Remove cookies with pancake turner. Cool on wire rack.

WHIZZ TRICK

For cookies with even more crunch, stir in ¼ cup chopped peanuts to the dough when the flour has been blended in.

By Jingo! Juice

Whenever Tom and Huck were planning a raft picnic, they used to concoct a special brew. They would pick fresh berries, mash them with sugar, and add just about anything that was handy. The result was so scrumptious that the only words to describe it were "By Jingo!"

SECRET INGREDIENTS

JELLY

2 LARGE ORANGES

GINGER ALE
PINT

ICE CUBES

MAGIC FORMULA

1. Squeeze the juice of _____ 1 orange
   Wash and cut the
   other orange into
   slices. Don't peel.

2. Mix together with _____ 4 tbsp blackberry
   in a large pitcher.   jelly (or juice
                         left over from
                         Blackberry Witches)

3. Add _____ 2 cups ginger ale
                         ice cubes

4. Stir well and serve at once. If not serving at once,
   leave out the ice cubes and ginger ale until the last
   minute.

Dinner with Davy Crockett

Having dinner with Davy Crockett isn't easy. For one thing, you can't sit down to dinner before you find it. There are no big supermarkets around to get your vittles from, and sometimes it takes a whole day to shoot a varmint big enough to fill the srewpot.

In winter, with the critters in hibernation, things are different. Then you'll get smoky bacon or salty pork for dinner. There'll be Indian pudding too or shoofly pie, leastways there will be if Davy can swap a few bearskins for sugar and spices.

But before you can sit down, there's a heap of wood to be chopped, cows to be milked, and pigs to be fed. After that, you're more'n welcome to be Davy's guest.

Mountain Soup

When there's no central heating in your old log cabin, nothing beats a bowl of hot bean soup for taking the chill off.

SECRET INGREDIENTS

MAGIC FORMULA

1. Put into deep saucepan _____ and simmer gently for ½ hour.

   1 can baked beans
   1 can consommé +
   1 can water
   1¼ tbsp onion flakes
   2½ tsp mild mustard
   1¼ tsp brown sugar
   1¼ tsp molasses

2. Add _____ 1 can tomatoes, mashed and simmer for 30 minutes more.

3. Serve piping hot.

Corn Fritters

If there's one thing they've got plenty of in Crockett country it's corn. You'll get corn pone, corn dodgers, hush puppies, mush biscuits, hoecake, hominy grits, and heaps of others. A favorite of Davy's is corn fritters, pipin' hot from the skillet. You can make them in a minute and they'll vanish just as quick!

SECRET INGREDIENTS

MAGIC FORMULA

1. Sift together into mixing bowl ___ ⅔ cup flour
   ½ tsp baking powder
   1½ tsp salt
   ¼ tsp pepper

2. In another bowl, beat until
   light in color _____ 1 egg
   then mix in _____ ½ cup milk

3. Make a well in the flour mixture.
   Gradually stir in egg
   mixture and _____ 1 cup kernel corn
   (drained)

4. Grease frying pan or griddle and place over medium heat.

5. When pan is hot, drop batter by teaspoonfuls (about 2 for each fritter). Fry until crisp and golden, turning once with a pancake turner.

6. Keep warm in oven (170°) until ready to serve.

Tennessee Taters

I reckon there are as many taters in Tennessee as there are ears o' corn. Open them up, spoon in a grate of cheese, a dollop of butter, and some crispy bacon. Then you're in for a treat — a real Tennessee tater.

SECRET INGREDIENTS

MAGIC FORMULA

1. Scrub clean _____ 4 baking potatoes

2. Bake in the oven at 400° for about 50 minutes or until potatoes feel soft when you stick a fork in them.

3. While potatoes are baking,
   fry until crispy _____ 4 slices bacon
   and drain on paper towel.

4. When potatoes are done, let them cool for a few minutes. Then, *wearing an oven mitt,* hold the potato with one hand and carefully cut a large cross into the potato skin with your other hand.

5. Using oven mitts, put one hand on either side of the potato and squeeze slightly so that the inside pushes out a little through the cross.

6. Carefully spoon _____ a dollop of
   into the opening, pressing   butter, and
   down firmly as you do it.   grated cheese

7. Sprinkle over the top _____ crumbled bacon

8. Fill the other 3 potatoes in the same way. Then put the potatoes under the broiler for 2 – 3 minutes to melt the cheese. Serve at once.

Raccoon Tails

If you've got your eye on Davy's hat, you'll be wanting to go chasing raccoon. But hold on a minute before you start heading for the out of doors. There's a way to track down a dozen or more a whole lot easier. Just rustle up a sugar and butter batter, with a splash of chocolate. In a short while, you'll have more raccoon tails than you can shake a stick at — 30 or more.

SECRET INGREDIENTS

FLOUR

GRANULATED SUGAR

BUTTER

LARGE

LEMON

CHOCOLATE SEMI-SWEET

BAKING POWDER

SALT

MAGIC FORMULA

1. Preheat oven to 375°, and grease a large cookie sheet.

2. In a large bowl, cream
together_____ 4½ tbsp soft butter
until light and fluffy. ½ cup sugar

3. Beat in _____ 1 egg
grated rind of
1 lemon

4. Sift in and mix well _____ 1 cup flour
1 tsp baking powder
pinch of salt

5. Drop dough by teaspoonfuls (1 tsp for each tail) on
greased cookie sheet.

6. Grease the back of the spoon;
dip it in sugar. Gently flatten the
tails. Add more sugar as needed.

7. Bake 7–9 minutes or until edges are light golden
brown. Remove from cookie sheet with pancake turner.

CHOCOLATE STRIPES

8. Melt in top of double boiler_____ 4 squares semisweet
over hot but not boiling chocolate
water. Stir until smooth, 3 tbsp butter
then remove from heat. 2½ tbsp water

9. Cool until mixture thickens slightly — about 15
minutes.

10. Chocolate should be thick enough to drip on cookies but
not run off edges. If
chocolate gets too thick,
heat and cool again.

Eskimorsels

If there is ever a time in your career of kitchen wizardry when you get all steamed up, don't dive into the deep freeze, head for the North Pole instead.

The Pole is the home of the whizz cream machine, an extraordinary ice-cream-making operation. Spies are sent in regularly from ice cream companies all over the world, but so far they have come out with only cold noses and empty hands. However, thanks to a friendly chef, a number of top Eskimorsel recipes have been smuggled out and are published here for the first time.

Polar Bear Sandwich

The problem with an outdoor storage system in the North Pole is that it tends to encourage polar bear picnics. Polar bear claws are tailor-made for prying the tops off containers and within minutes three or four gallons of the choicest ice cream can be gobbled up.

One recipe in particular seems to be their favorite and it is now known as Polar Bear Sandwich.

SECRET INGREDIENTS

SANDWICH COOKIES 20

HEAVY CREAM ½ PINT

MILK

BUTTER

24 WHITE MARSHMALLOWS

PEPPERMINT EXTRACT

MAGIC FORMULA

1. Line a 9-inch loaf pan with aluminum foil.

2. Melt together in double boiler_____ over hot water, stirring from time to time.
   24 white marshmallows
   ½ cup milk

3. Remove pan from heat and stir in _____ Put into refrigerator to cool slightly.
   2½ tsp peppermint extract

4. Put into plastic bag _____ Tie tightly, and crush to crumbs with rolling pin.
   20 chocolate sandwich cookies

5. In a bowl that has been chilled in the refrigerator, whip _____ 1 cup heavy cream until soft peaks form.
   Then fold into marshmallow mixture with metal spoon.

6. Cover bottom of loaf pan with light sprinkling of crumbs. Then cover with a layer of marshmallow mixture, a layer of crumbs, another layer of marshmallow. Finish up with a layer of crumbs.

7. Cover with foil and put into the freezer overnight.

8. To serve, turn upside down onto a plate. Take off foil and slice as you would a loaf of bread.

Igloodle

Another North Pole treat is the completely edible igloo, made of squares of crispy cereal and marshmallow.

If the squares get too hard to work with when you're building your Igloodle, just put them into the oven for a few minutes and they'll soften up.

SECRET INGREDIENTS

CRISPY CEREAL

30 WHITE MARSHMALLOWS

BUTTER

VANILLA

MAGIC FORMULA

1. Grease a 9-inch baking pan.

2. Melt in a large saucepan_____ 30 white marshmallows
   over low heat, stirring all   3 tbsp. butter
   the time to prevent sticking.

3. When completely melted, take off
   the heat and add_____ 1¼ tsp vanilla

4. Then stir in quickly_____ 5 cups crispy cereal
   and mix thoroughly.

5. Put into greased pan. When cool enough to handle,
   press down evenly with your fingers.

6. Cut into squares (make 25 squares) then take out the
   squares one by one to construct the igloo.

7. Form a small circle of squares
   (about 7) on a cookie sheet.
   Fix two squares pointing out
   for the doorway.

   Build another layer on top, pressing squares together
   to seal. When you get to the third layer, slant
   the squares over slightly and press together. Use
   one square to close the roof and two squares to
   cover the doorway.

8. Use as an edible party
   decoration. Or fill
   with ice cream and slice
   as you would a pie.

Lemon Whizz Cream

One day every month, the whizz cream machine is switched on to Lemon Whizz Cream and in no time it produces this most delicious ice cream. It is the best polar medicine yet invented.

SECRET INGREDIENTS

MAGIC FORMULA

1. Cut in half and squeeze the
   juice of _____ 2 lemons

2. Strain juice into a small bowl
   and beat together with _____ 2 egg yolks
   pinch of salt

3. In another bowl that has been chilled in
   the refrigerator, beat until standing in
   soft peaks _____ 1 cup heavy
   cream

4. With metal spoon, fold in _____ 3 tbsp sugar

5. In third bowl, beat until stiff _____ 2 egg whites
   then fold in _____ ½ cup sugar

6. Fold lemon-egg mixture into the whipped cream. Then
   fold the beaten egg whites into the whipped cream.

7. When completely blended, pour into a plastic container
   with a lid and put in the freezer overnight.

WHIZZ TRICK

For special occasions, pour Whizz Cream into a round
container lined with aluminum foil. Freeze overnight.
Then, just before serving, turn upside down on a plate.
Remove the foil, and decorate with whipped cream,
colored sparkles, or chocolate sprinkles.

Milk Snozzle

Eski-kids pride themselves on the endless Milk Snozzle drinks they can make. They have listed a few here for you to try. Change the flavors to suit your taste, then follow the MAGIC FORMULA.

Shake up:

Milk - blueberries - vanilla ice cream

Milk - orange juice - vanilla ice cream

Milk - mashed peaches - vanilla ice cream

Milk - chocolate syrup - chocolate ice cream

Milk - mashed banana - vanilla ice cream

Milk - raspberries - vanilla ice cream

Milk - strawberries - strawberry ice cream

SECRET INGREDIENTS

MILK

MAGIC FORMULA

1. Put into a large clean jar _____ and screw the top on tightly.

½ cup cold milk
2½ tbsp fruit or chocolate syrup
1 large scoop of ice cream

2. Using both hands, shake the jar back and forth vigorously for a minute.

3. Pour into a tall glass and sip through a straw!